Using
PowerPoint 2003

CW01395149

Other Titles of Interest

Using Microsoft PowerPoint 2003

David Weale

Bernard Babani (Publishing) Ltd

The Grampians

Shepherds Bush Road

London W6 7NF

England

www.babanibooks.com

Please Note

Although every care has been taken with the production of this book to ensure that any instructions or any of the other contents operate in a correct and safe manner, the Author and the Publishers do not accept any responsibility for any failure, damage or loss caused by following the said contents. The Author and Publisher do not take any responsibility for errors or omissions.

The Author and Publisher make no warranty or representation, either express or implied, with respect to the contents of this book, its quality, merchantability or fitness for a particular purpose.

The Author and Publisher will not be liable to the purchaser or to any other person or legal entity with respect to any liability, loss or damage (whether direct, indirect, special, incidental or consequential) caused or alleged to be caused directly or indirectly by this book.

The book is sold as is, without any warranty of any kind, either expressed or implied, respecting the contents, including but not limited to implied warranties regarding the book's quality, performance, correctness or fitness for any particular purpose.

No part of this book may be reproduced or copied by any means whatever without written permission of the publisher.

Preface

Welcome, I wrote this book to help you to learn how to use the program in a practical way. It is intended to explain the program in a way that I hope you will find useful.

Each section of the book covers a different aspect of the program and contains various hints and tips which I have found useful and may enhance your work.

Features for this new edition include:

☐ Tutorial and explanation of the techniques contained in the program

☐ Glossary

☐ An expanded section on presentation techniques

☐ Keyboard shortcuts

The text is written both for the new user and for the more experienced person who wants an easy to follow reference.

You should know how to use the basic techniques of Microsoft® Windows®; if you do not, there are many excellent texts on the subject.

I hope you learn from this book and have fun doing so.

David Weale, March 2004

Trademarks

Microsoft®, Windows® XP and PowerPoint 2003 are registered trademarks of Microsoft ® Corporation.

All other trademarks are the registered and legally protected trademarks of the companies who make the products. There is no intent to use the trademarks generally moreover; readers should investigate ownership of a trademark before using it for any purpose.

About the author

David Weale is a Fellow of the Institute of Chartered Accountants and has worked in both private and public practice, presently he is a lecturer in business computing and statistics.

Contents

Starting Off

To use **Microsoft® PowerPoint 2003**, click the icon on the **Desktop** or on the **Quick Launch** toolbar (next to the **Start** button).

Alternatively click the **Start** button, select **All Programs** and then **Microsoft Office**, followed by **Microsoft Office PowerPoint 2003**.

The display

When you load for the first time, you will see the screen shown below.

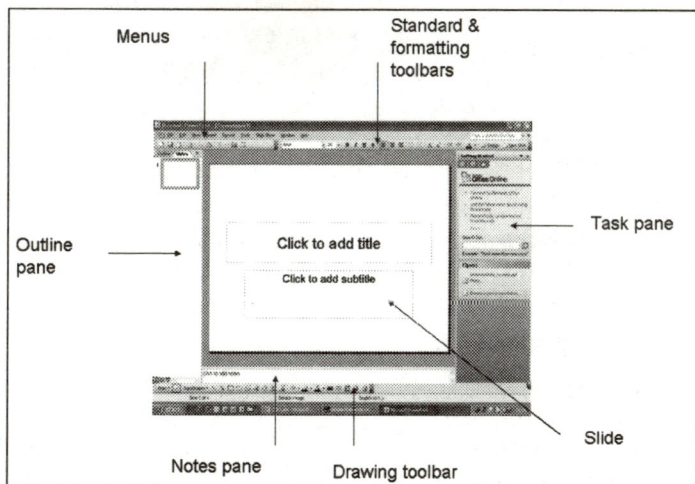

The **Standard**, **Formatting** and **Drawing** toolbar(s) contain buttons to carry out activities or commands.

The default setting is to display a single line of toolbar buttons at the top of the screen, plus the **Drawing** toolbar along the bottom of the screen, the **Task Pane** toolbar to the right of the screen, the **Outline** pane to the left and the **Notes** pane along the bottom of the screen.

To display any toolbar, pull down the **View** menu, select **Toolbars** and then the chosen toolbar.

Tip

To show the **Standard** & **Formatting** toolbar buttons in two rows, click the arrow (**Toolbar Options**) at the end of the toolbar and select **Show Buttons on Two Rows.** The display will change to show two lines of toolbars.

Position the mouse pointer over any of the toolbar buttons and a description will appear (called **ScreenTips**, this is an option that can be turned off if you wish – **Tools, Customize, Options**).

Click the right-hand mouse button while pointing at any button and a pull-down menu showing the available toolbars appears, these can be displayed or hidden.

The Panes

There are various panes to assist you.

The **Outline** pane (left of the screen) displays a small representation of each slide *or* the outline text for each slide (switch between these views using the buttons at the top of the pane).

The **Task** pane (on the right of the screen) displays tasks that can be carried out by clicking the appropriate item, the contents of the pane change with the activity.

The **Notes** pane is useful; use it to enter text you want to use (to help you) within your presentation, i.e. prompts, details, etc. The **Notes Pages** can be printed out (using **Print** within the **File** menu and selecting **Notes** in the **Print What** box) and used during the presentation.

Removing the panes

The **Outline** and **Task** panes can be removed by clicking the **X** button (on the top right of the pane).

To restore the **Task** pane, pull down the **View** menu and select **Task Pane** from the list.

Tip

Resize the **Notes** pane (bottom of screen) by clicking and dragging the divide along the top of the pane.

The pull-down menus

Along the top of the screen are the pull-down menus.

When you click the (left) mouse button on any of these, a menu will appear. Each menu contains commands (some of which can also be carried out more quickly using the toolbar buttons).

Quick Start

The following section covers the main elements of the program so that you can quickly produce a presentation.

To begin a presentation

Pulling down the **File** menu, followed by **New** will begin a new presentation by displaying the **New Presentation** pane on the right of the screen.

New

There are four choices (shown in the pane).

Note the **arrows** and **home** buttons at the top; these make it easy to move between the different **Task panes**.

Blank Presentation

The initial option is the blank presentation. This gives you a choice of text layouts (shown in the **Task** pane on the right of the screen) without the addition of a design.

There is a variety of different types of layouts, which can be changed at any time (if the **Slide** Layout pane is not shown then pull down the **Format** menu and select **Slide Layout**).

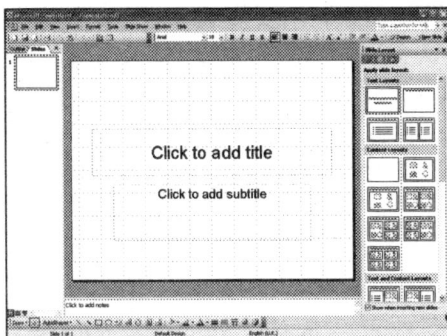

This is the best choice if you wish to apply a design at a later stage; although it is better to begin with your chosen design rather than impose it later on, as different templates contain different font designs and sizes.

From design template

It is a sensible idea to select the design early in the process of designing your slide show as each design imposes colour schemes and font choices, which may affect the amount of text on a slide.

Use the scrollbar (on the right) to see the choices and select one by clicking it; it will then be imposed onto your slide(s). Note the very last choice, the **Microsoft** web site has additional templates, which can be previewed and downloaded.

Design Templates on Microsoft Office Online

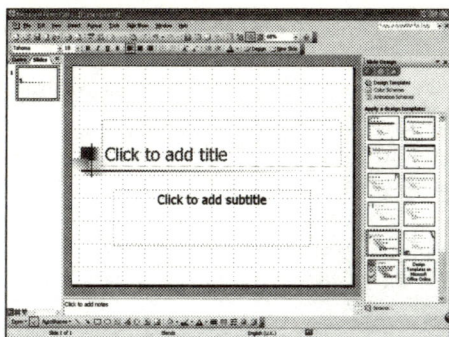

Right-clicking (or clicking the arrow to the right) the designs gives three choices, **Show Large Previews** can be useful to enable more clarity and the design can be applied to the current slide or to all the slides.

From AutoContent wizard

This guides you through a series of steps. The result is a professional looking presentation created in a very short time, the only drawback being that it will be similar in style to any other presentation created using the wizard (however, it is easy to customise).

The initial dialog box is shown below.

This is followed by a series of dialog boxes. As can be seen from the following illustration, there are a variety of different presentations from which to choose.

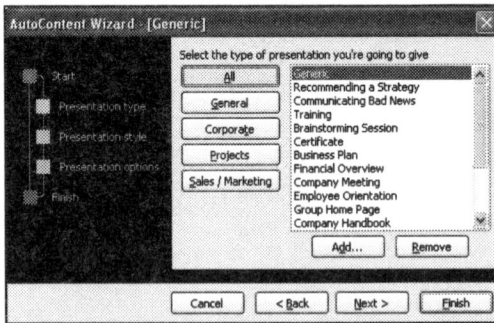

When you have finished, the Wizard leaves you with a presentation with prompting text already in place.

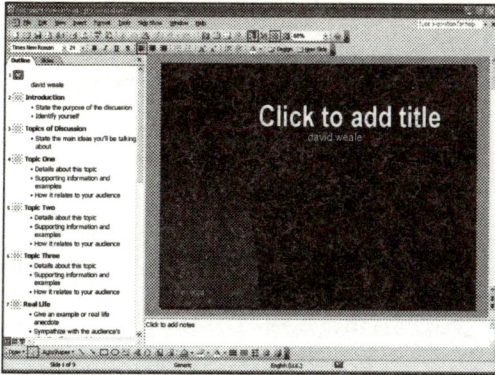

Finally, alter the text (by highlighting and overwriting) to whatever you want to say. You can add or delete slides as you wish and customise the colours, fonts, design, etc.

From existing presentation

An existing slide show can be used as the basis for the new presentations, the existing file will be opened and then you can add or delete slides, change the content, design, etc., and save it under a new name.

Templates

There is a choice of template.

Templates on Office Online

This links to the Microsoft web site and displays a choice of templates, select one of these and it will become the background to your presentation.

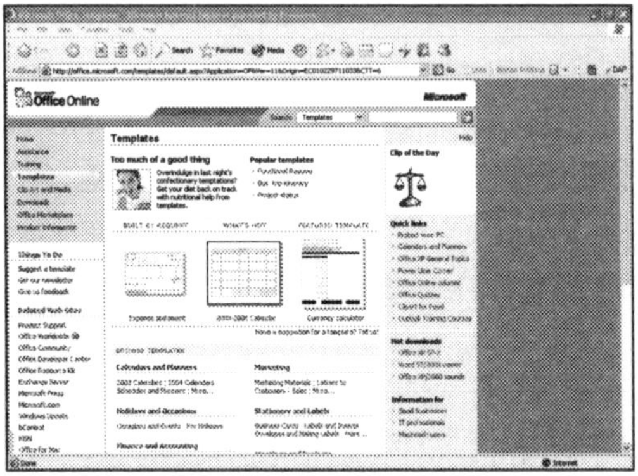

The site contains templates, which are *downloadable* so you can save them and use them again without having to revisit the site.

An example is shown below, note that I entered PowerPoint in the search criteria (top right of the screen) as templates are available for all Office programs and this narrows down the list.

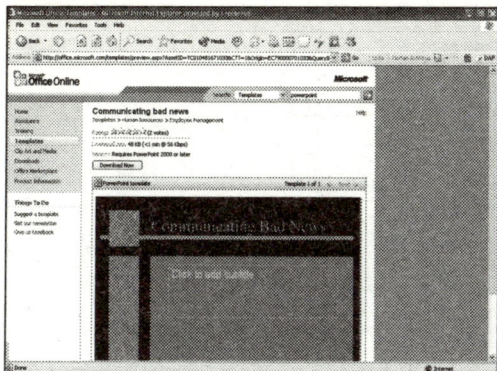

Tip

The site is updated regularly and it is worthwhile revisiting this site.

On my computer/web sites

Using this option, you can look for templates on your hard disc (that have been installed with the program or downloaded from the Microsoft site) or from your web sites.

The dialog boxes are shown below; the first is an alternative to using **From Design Templates**, the second displays existing presentations, which you adapt and alter as necessary (an alternative to using the **AutoContent Wizard**, this option is quicker but gives less control over the finished result).

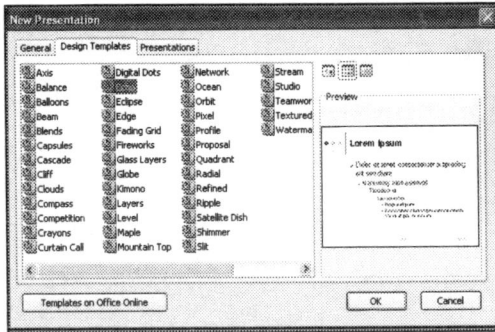

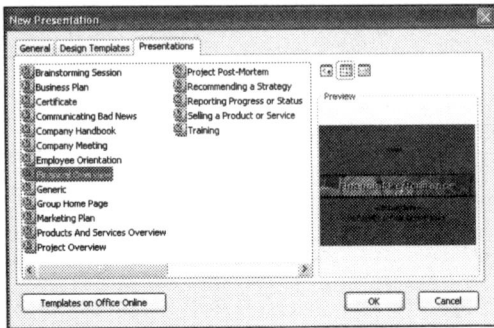

Tip

If you are going to use the same format for several presentations (e.g. company logo), create a *template* with all the logos and formatting in place, this will save considerable time.

To add a new slide

Use the **New Slide** button (on the toolbar) to add a new slide (which will appear after the current slide).

Alternatively, pull down the **Insert** menu and select **New Slide**, or use the keys **Ctrl** and **M** to achieve the same result.

Moving between slides

There are several ways to move from one slide to another.

☐ Click the required slide in the **Outline** pane (to the left of the screen).

☐ Use the keyboard **Pg Up** and **Pg Dn**.

☐ Use the scroll-bar to the right of the actual slide.

Changing the design

Click the **Design** button (on the **Formatting** toolbar) to display the **Slide Design** pane on the right of the screen. This will display the choices (use the scrollbar to move through them).

The **Slide Design** pane includes options to change the **Color Scheme** and **Animation Scheme** (animations are covered later in the text).

Color Scheme

This option displays the choices in the right-hand pane. Moving the mouse pointer over any of the schemes displays an arrow (on the right of the colour scheme); click this to apply the colour scheme.

Show Large Previews is useful and the colour schemes can be applied to the *current* or *selected* slides (select them in **Slide Sorter View**) or to *all* the slides.

There is also an **Edit Color Schemes** link at the bottom of the pane (this loads a dialog box in which the colours can be changed).

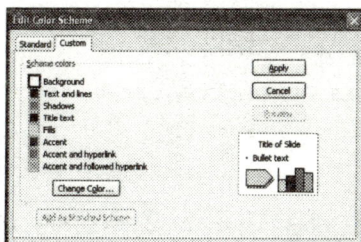

Looking at Your Slides

Along the bottom left of the screen are three buttons enabling the slides to be looked at in different ways (there are further views available from the **View** pull-down menu).

From left to right the buttons are **Normal** view, **Slide Sorter** view and **Slide Show** view.

Normal View

The default view and the view used to create the slides.

Sizing the panes

The panes can be sized (click and drag the divider between the sections of the screen) and closed (using the **Close** button that appears top right on every window).

Zooming

To size (*any*) display, click the **Zoom** button on the upper toolbar.

Alternatively, pull down the **View** menu and choose **Zoom**, this gives more control as you can enter a figure in the **Percent** box.

Slide Sorter View

You can look at all the slides by clicking on the **Slide Sorter View** button.

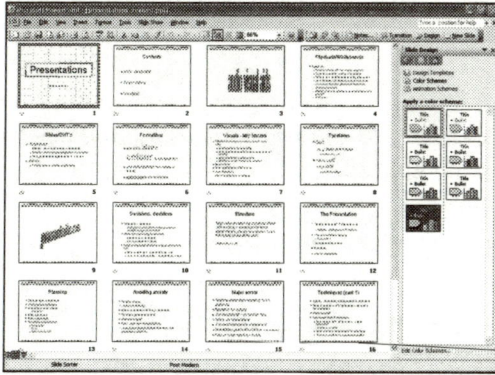

This displays (small) images of all the slides and they can be rearranged in sequence or added/deleted.

To move the slides around, click on a slide with the mouse and then drag it to a new position between two slides (a line will appear between the slides).

In **Slide Sorter View** use **Select All** from the **Edit** menu and apply special effects such as **Transitions** to all the slides (using the **Transition** button on the toolbar).

Slide Show

View the slide show as it would appear (projected onto a screen) by clicking on the **Slide Show** button (bottom of the screen).

Tip

Using a projector is the most effective way of presenting and you can build in special effects such as **Transitions** and **Animations** (which is not possible if the slides are printed onto overhead transparencies).

The Slide Show menu

There are many features available during a slide show. Click the right-hand mouse button during a slide show, to display the following menu.

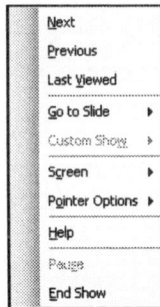

```
Next
Previous
Last Viewed
.......................
Go to Slide         ▶
Custom Show         ▶
.......................
Screen              ▶
Pointer Options     ▶
.......................
Help
.......................
Pause
End Show
```

The most important of these are explained.

Next/Previous/Last Viewed/Go to Slide

Use these commands to move to the next or previous point or slide.

Custom Show

This jumps to a custom show (you have to have created a custom show - **Slide Show** and **Custom Shows**).

Screen

Use this option to change the look, or to display (or add) speaker notes or minutes during the presentation.

Pointer Options

You can change the arrow to write on the screen (whether this is legible depends upon your mouse control).

End Show

This ends the presentation abruptly.

Toolbar

When the slide show is run, the new Slide Show toolbar appears on the bottom left of the screen to provide easy navigation.

Tip

I suggest you end the slide show either with a black screen or have a final slide that you can leave while you answer questions, for example your company logo. This is more professional than just ending the show and reverting to the program.

Printing

To print your file, click on the **Print** button on the upper toolbar, this prints to the default printer.

If you pull down the **File** menu and select **Print,** you will see the following dialog box that offers you various choices.

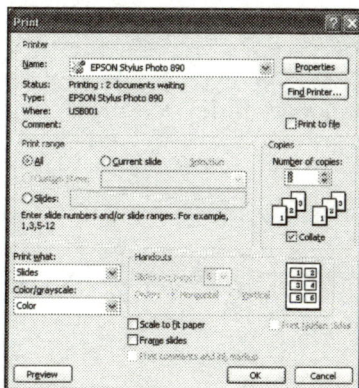

Print what

There is a choice of what to print.

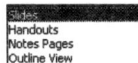

Slides

This prints the individual slides, one to a page.

Handouts

Select **Handouts** (1, 2, 3, 4, 6 or 9 slides per page) to print off audience handouts, which give your audience both something to annotate during the presentation and to take away.

Notes Pages

The slides and your notes are printed for each slide.

Outline View

Prints the outline view, i.e. the contents of the **Outline Pane** – this is the text of the slides without any formatting.

There are also more printing options in the (bottom of) the dialog box.

Scale to fit paper

This alters the scale of the slides to fit the paper size being used.

Frame slides

This prints a frame around each slide.

Print comments and ink markup

Prints the comments you have added to individual slides (see *comments*) and any handwritten comments you have made using a tablet pen.

A Tablet PC is a computer running Microsoft Windows XP Tablet PC Edition; this allows you to write on the screen using a tablet pen.

Print hidden slides

You can hide slides within your presentation (so they do not appear when the slide show is run). If this option is selected, they will be included in the printout.

Saving Your Work

Tip

Get into the habit of saving your work regularly so that any problems, whether hardware or software, do not cause too much loss of time or other problems. It is best to save to the **hard disc,** as floppy discs are not as reliable.

If the **AutoRecover** feature is set then, in the event of a system failure, you will only be a few minutes from your last version (**Tools, Options, Save**). Personally, I set this feature *and* save the file regularly.

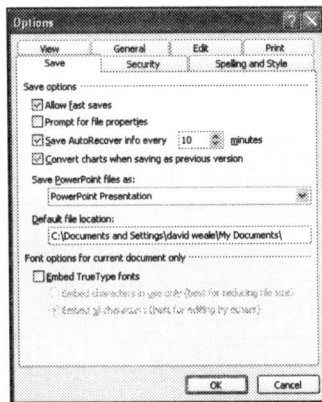

To save your work you can click on the **Save** button on the toolbar along the top of the screen. Change where you save the file by clicking on the arrow to the right of **Save in** and alter the folder or disc (use the buttons to locate the folder).

Next time the **Save** button is clicked, the process will be automatic and no dialog box will appear.

If (after the initial saving) you want to save to a different folder or filename then pull down the **File** menu and select **Save As**.

Tips

☐ The **Save as type** option enables you to save your file in a variety of different formats so that it can be opened in another program or an earlier version of the program (if you save it as an earlier version, some features that exist in PowerPoint 2003 may not be available).

☐ Any presentation created in Microsoft PowerPoint 95, PowerPoint 97, PowerPoint 2000, or PowerPoint 2002 can be opened in PowerPoint 2003.

☐ Remember to **backup** your presentation files to another media; this can be a floppy disc or preferably a CDR or CDRW.

Text

Entering Text

This is simple, click within the slide where prompted and begin typing.

When entering text use the *return* key to move on to the next point.

Altering the Font

Each design has fonts allocated to it, often these are ideal, but if you want to alter the fonts, there are several methods.

☐ Highlight the text (by clicking and dragging the mouse to select the text), then click on the **Font** button along the upper toolbar and choose another font.

☐ You can also alter the **Font Size** in the same way.

☐ Alternatively, highlight the text, pull down the **Format** menu, and select **Font**, this gives more choices.

Tips

☐ If you alter the **Master Slide**, the text within all the slides in the file changes to the new font/font size (see section on *master slides*).

☐ To see the actual fonts in the font selection of the formatting toolbar, pull down the **Tools** menu, select **Customize** and **Options** tab, and click **List font names in their font**.

Spell Checking Your Text

It is very easy to destroy the professionalism of your presentation by using incorrect spelling.

Click the button along the upper toolbar and the spellchecking dialog box will appear.

The way a spell checker operates is to compare every word you enter against a (finite) list of words. If the word you type is not in the list, the spell checker program will identify it. This does not mean it is wrong; merely that it is not in the dictionary.

You can **Add** words to your dictionary if you wish.

Graphics & Objects

It is useful and rewarding to add visuals to your presentation. You can add:

- ☐ Clip Art (from the library that comes with the program)

- ☐ Pictures, sound and video clips

- ☐ Graphs

- ☐ WordArt

- ☐ Tables

- ☐ Organisation Charts

- ☐ Other objects

Clip Art

Choose the slide to which you want to add the image.

Click on the **Clip Art** button on the **Drawing** toolbar (which should appear along the bottom of the screen, if it does not then pull down the **View** menu, select **Toolbars**, followed by **Drawing**).

The **Clip Art** pane will appear on the right of the screen. This can be used to search for relevant items by entering keywords in the **Search text** box and clicking the **Search** button. The results are then shown (use the scrollbars to see all the items).

Tip

Select **Everywhere** in the **Search In** box (menu), this will connect with the Microsoft website and display additional items (right-click any of these to add them to your own collection by choosing **Make Available Offline**).

To insert the item, click the arrow to the right of the item; this will display a menu from which you select, e.g. **Copy** or **Insert**.

Pictures, sounds and videos

Photographs, sounds and motion (video) clips can be added to your slide show and are included within the gallery.

To search for specific types of media (e.g. sounds), click the **Results should be: (Insert Clip Art** pane) and ensure only those media types are clicked.

Graphs

You can create and insert graphs by clicking on the toolbar button.

This loads **Microsoft Graph** (an application that can be accessed from all the main applications, e.g. **PowerPoint** or **Word**). You create your own graph by altering and/or adding to the data shown.

When the chart is selected, new buttons appear on the toolbar (the **View Datasheet** button is only visible if you show the toolbar buttons on two rows). Change the graph by using the buttons, graphs can be sized and so on in a similar way to other visuals.

To alter a graph, double-click it and you can then edit it as you wish by using the various features of the **Graph** application.

Tip

You can import data from a spreadsheet program such as **Excel** or insert an existing graph from **Excel** by using the **Insert** (**Object**) pull-down menu (or **Paste** a graph from the originating program). This is the preferred option as **Excel** gives far more choices and can produce very sophisticated graphs and charts.

WordArt

Another object you can insert into your presentation is **WordArt**. You can use this to create special text effects and fancy lettering for logos or titles.

Click the **Insert WordArt** button (**Drawing** toolbar) to begin the process; you will see the following screen.

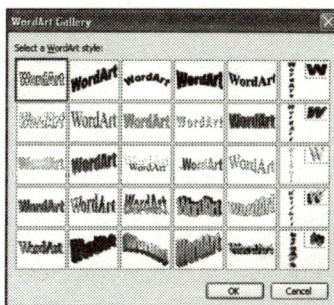

Select the style you want (you can change it later) and click **OK**, the screen will show a text entry box.

Enter your text in the box (returning to create a new line) and then use the buttons to create the effect you want.

The text can be altered using the **WordArt** toolbar.

To alter your **WordArt** object double-click it and **WordArt** will be loaded again.

Tables

Tables are very useful to lay out text or images in columns.

Creating tables within PowerPoint

Insert a new slide, choosing the **Table** layout (as shown in the illustration) from the **Slide Layout** pane (scroll down until it appears).

Double-click the icon and decide how many rows and columns you want (you can add or delete them at a later stage if necessary).

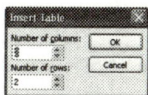

Another method is to pull down the **Insert** menu and select **Table**; this will display the **Insert Table** dialog box (above).

Alternatively, click the **Table** button, this lets you highlight the number of rows and columns you want in your table.

Whichever method is used, a table will appear, along with the **Tables** toolbar, which can be used to create various effects.

Tips

☐ Use **Borders and Fills** to create effects within the tables. To do this highlight the cells, pull down the **Table** menu from the **Tables and Borders** toolbar and select **Borders and Fills**, alternatively select the cells and right-click the mouse, then choose **Borders and Fills**.

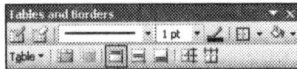

☐ Sometimes it may be preferable to create a table in **Word** and then **Paste** it into **PowerPoint**, **Word** contains more powerful and sophisticated features.

Organisation Charts

One of the advantages of a program such as **PowerPoint** is the variety of pre-designed diagrams and other graphics available.

To insert an organisation chart into your presentation, use the slide layout (**Slide Layout** pane).

After selecting this, you will see the slide, double-click the symbol and you can begin to create your organisation chart.

There is a choice of charts, which are described in the **Diagram Gallery** that appears.

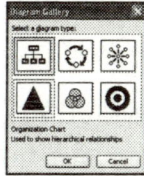

Select the first of these and the **Microsoft Organization Chart** module will appear.

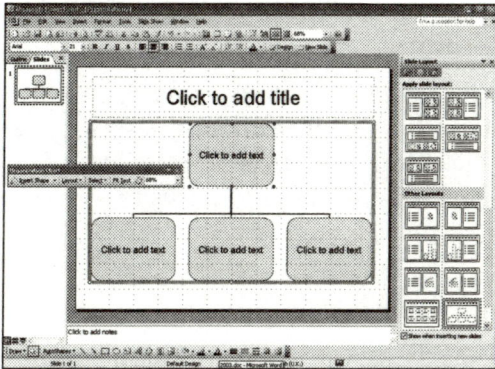

Enter the names and titles by clicking the relevant box and typing, the boxes can be added to or deleted.

Organization Chart Toolbar

The toolbar extends the functionality of the chart.

Tip

The (down) arrow on the title bar of the toolbar enables you to **Add or Remove Buttons** from the toolbar or to **Customize** the contents of the toolbar (all toolbars allow customisation in this way).

Insert Shape

Use **Insert Shape** to add boxes to the chart by selecting a box and then clicking **Insert Shape.** Click the down arrow to the right of the **Insert Shape** button to display the choices.

Layout

Click the arrow on the button to display the variety of layout formatting tools to apply to the organisation chart.

Select

The **Select** button enables all or part of the chart to be selected (click and drag the mouse to achieve the same effect).

Fit Text

Use this button to fit the text into the boxes, it
has the effect of reducing the size of (all) the
text to fit the boxes.

`Fit Text`

AutoFormat

This is a quick and easy way to apply formatting
to the chart.

Choose the effect you want and it will be imposed onto the
chart.

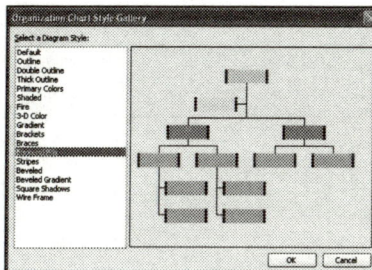

Other Objects

There are several other objects you can add to your presentation, e.g. **Microsoft Equation 3** (using this you can enter very complex mathematical symbols and equations).

To access these, pull down the **Insert** menu, followed by **Object** and select from the list.

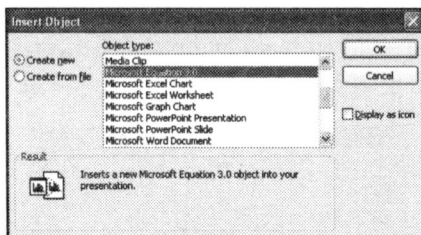

Artwork

Manipulating Images

There are various techniques to manipulate (most) images.

Moving an Image (or Other Object)

Make sure that the image has been selected, then click the mouse within the image (it becomes a four-headed cross) and while holding down the mouse button drag the image to a new position.

Sizing an Image

There are two ways to achieve this.

□ Select the image and position the mouse pointer on one of the corners of the image. The mouse pointer will become a small line with arrows at either end. Keeping the mouse button held down, move the mouse to resize the image.

□ Alternatively, select the image (by clicking it), pull down the **Format** menu, and select **Picture** (**Object** or **WordArt**). In the dialog box enter the percentage (in the **Size** tab) to scale to (right-clicking the object and selecting **Format** from the displayed list may be even quicker).

Cropping an Object

Cropping is different from sizing.

Sizing makes the whole image smaller (or bigger); cropping an object removes part of the whole object from view.

This is sometimes useful to remove extraneous parts of a picture or other image.

To do this, display the **Picture** toolbar and the cropping tool will be shown (the toolbar may appear automatically when you select the image, if it does not, pull down the **View** menu, selecting **Toolbars**).

Using the mouse, select the tool, grab any corner or side of your object with the tool and remove part of the object.

Tip

Bring back any part of a cropped image in the same way it was removed, it is only removed from view, not actually deleted.

Customising Slides

This section deals with the methods of customising your presentation so that it stands out from other presentations.

The Master Slide

Make changes to all the slides by amending the **Master** slide.

To do this, pull down the **View** menu, select **Master** and choose the type of master from the list.

Any changes or additions will be reflected in all the slides *of that style* (i.e. if you have changed the **Slide Master** this will not affect the **Title** slide).

However, it may be necessary to change each slide individually as this may not work in certain circumstances, e.g. files created with older versions of the program

Tip

It is best to create your master slide layout (including transitions, animations, etc.) before creating the slide show, as your choices will affect the number of lines and number of characters on each line.

Deleting Slides

There are two ways to achieve this:

☐ In **Normal View** pull down the **Edit** menu and then select **Delete Slide**.

☐ In **Slide Sorter View** select the slide or slides by clicking on them and press the **Delete** key.

Tip

Clicking the initial slide and then holding down the **Shift** key while clicking the last slide (you want to select) will select all those slides. Using the **Ctrl** key and clicking enables non-sequential slides to be selected.

Drawing toolbar

If you are doing any work with graphics, then you will want to display the **Drawing** toolbar. I work with it permanently displayed. There are some very useful tools here, for example, you can add text boxes and arrows to any part of your slides

Tip

To display any toolbar, pull down the **View** menu and select **Toolbars**, click on your choice. The toolbar will be displayed.

Draw

Use this option to display the various options explained below.

Grouping and Ungrouping

Ungrouping divides the image into its component parts, however, it is not possible to ungroup certain types of image (although this version of the program may be able to convert the image into a **Microsoft Office drawing object** and enable it to be ungrouped).

To ungroup an image, select it and then choose **Ungroup** (select **Draw** from the **Drawing** toolbar).

The image will now be made up of many sub-images all with little squares surrounding them (the image shown in the illustration was created using **AutoShapes** from the **Drawing** toolbar). Click outside the image and then click on any sub-image and move it, recolour it, size it or delete it as you wish (it may also be possible to ungroup a sub-image).

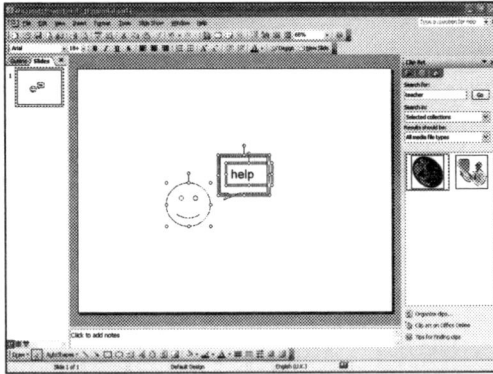

Tip

To select more than one component or object, hold down the **Shift** key while clicking the mouse on each item you want to select.

Merging images

You can join several images into one so that they form a single group, which can then be moved or resized. Below are the alternative methods to achieve this.

☐ Hold down the mouse button and drag the mouse around the items.

☐ While holding down the **Shift** key, click the mouse on each item you want to include within the group *or*

☐ Pull down the **Edit** menu and choose **Select All**.

Finally, (whichever method is used) choose **Group** or **Regroup** from the **Draw** menu to combine all the images.

Order

If you place one object on top of another, the order in which these can be displayed can be critical to the result.

It is useful to think of the objects as being stacked, one on top of the next (in a similar way to a pack of cards).

The commands to vary the sequence are:

Bring to Front

This brings the selected object to the *top* of the pile.

Send to Back

This sends the selected object to the *bottom* of the pile.

Bring Forward

This brings the selected object *forward* one level in the pile.

Send Backward

This sends the selected object *back* one level in the pile.

Grid and Guides

There is an (invisible) grid and any object or text aligns itself to this. It makes lining up easier to achieve but does reduce fine control.

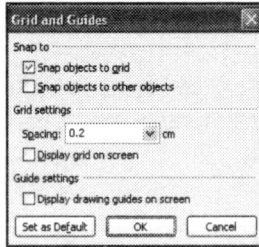

This dialog box can be used to display the gridlines (or guides).

The illustration below shows the screen with both the **grid** and the **drawing guides** shown (the **drawing guides** can be moved around the screen by clicking and dragging).

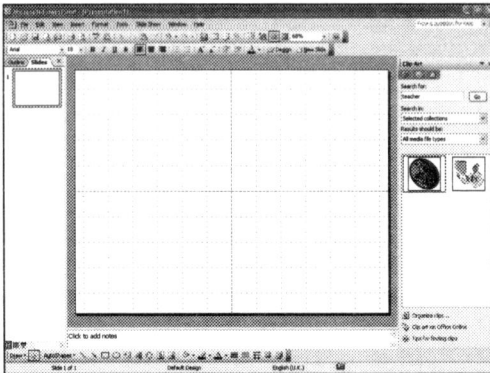

Nudge

After an object has been selected, it can be nudged up, down or sideways.

Align or Distribute

This can be used to align objects and/or text. Select *more* than one object or text, and then pull down the **Draw** menu and **Align or Distribute**. The objects will then be aligned together (this is much easier than attempting to align objects manually).

Save the file before making any experimental changes to it.

Rotate or Flip

Selected objects or text can be rotated or flipped within **PowerPoint**.

To do so, select the **Draw** menu, select **Rotate or Flip**.

Free Rotate lets you grab any of the corners with the rotate tool and rotate to your heart's desire.

If your image will not allow the choice of **Rotate or Flip** then it may be possible to **Ungroup** it (**Draw** menu) and then **Group** it again, it then becomes a **PowerPoint** object, which can be rotated.

Edit Points

If you have created a freeform shape (e.g. by using any of the freeform tools (shown opposite) in the **AutoShapes Lines**), you can then move or edit the points within that object.

Change AutoShape

If you have created an **AutoShape**, and you select this option (while the **AutoShape** object is still selected) then you can choose another shape and the original shape will be converted into the new one.

AutoShapes

The **AutoShapes** menu is shown below.

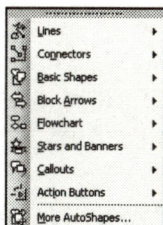

Select the symbol, then click, and drag to produce the shape.

Once this has been done, the image can be manipulated, e.g. the shape or the colour can be changed.

PowerPoint and the Web

With the growing importance and use of the Internet, all the **Microsoft Office** programs contain web tools.

These tools enable files to be converted into a format that can be used on the Internet or company Intranets without the need for extensive knowledge of HTML coding.

Saving a presentation as HTML

To save the presentation as a web site, pull down the **File** menu and select **Save as Web Page**.

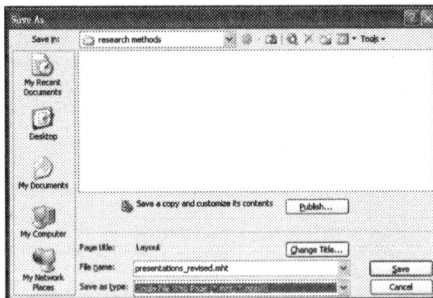

The default setting saves the file with a .MHT extension; this is a single file containing all the slides in the presentation. The following illustration shows the file opened in the browser.

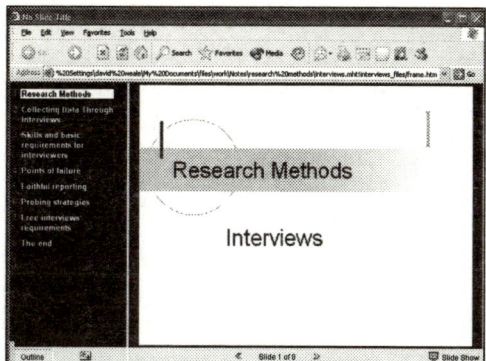

Click the slide names (on the left of the screen) to see each individual slide or click the **Slide Show** button on the (bottom) right, the slide show will be run (click the **Outline** button to close the outline pane).

Alternatively, using the **Publish** button allows various options to be set *before* saving the file.

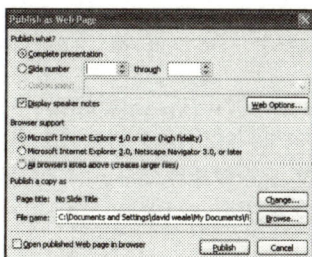

Tips

☐ Pay attention to the **All browsers listed above**. While this will increase the file size, the file will work across a wide platform of browsers (clicking the **Publish** button saves the file as a series of web pages in their own named folder).

☐ Clicking the **Open published Web page in browser**, means the browser will be loaded and the pages displayed without any further intervention on your part.

☐ This version of the program stores the whole presentation in one file rather than as a series of HTML files (as in the previous versions); this saves disc space. If you prefer the previous method, pull down the **Save as type** list to save it in the form **Web Page** (this creates an index page and a folder containing a file for each of the pages within the presentation).

Adding hyperlinks to a presentation

Hyperlinks can be added to a slide, as an **Action Button** (explained later) or as a normal hyperlink (which will work when you run the **Slide Show**) so that you can jump to another slide or to an Internet link.

To do this, highlight the text or select an object and click the **Insert Hyperlink** button on the toolbar, finally enter the necessary data into the dialog box.

The Menus

This section of the book deals with the commands in the pull-down menus that have not been dealt with previously.

Tips

□ There is an arrow at the bottom of the pull-down menus; this means that there are additional commands, which are accessed by clicking the arrow.

□ It is possible to set the full menus to appear as the *default* by using the **Tools** menu, followed by **Customize** and **Options** and ticking **Always show full menus**.

File menu

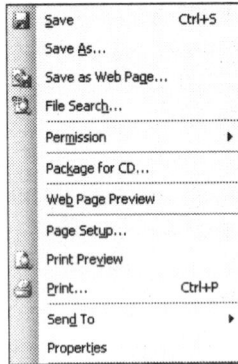

Save / Save As

These save the file (**Save As** gives the option to alter the file name or folder).

Tips

☐ If the file size seems to keep increasing, use **Save As** giving the file a new name, this may reduce the file size by up to half.

☐ Turn off **Fast Saves** (**Tools**, **Options**, **Save**) this makes the files smaller (useful when emailing or saving to a floppy disc).

☐ Turn off **Save preview picture** (**File**, **Properties**, and **Summary**); this reduces the file size.

File Search

A new feature, this enables a search for files containing specified text. The search can be narrowed using **Other Search Options** and there is an **Advanced File Search** available (bottom of pane).

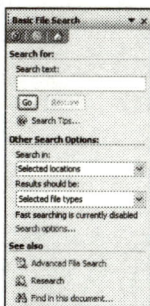

The search results in a list of files, any of which can be opened by clicking the filename.

This is a very powerful and *useful* feature (as everyone mislays files at some point or cannot remember which folder they are stored within).

Permission

A new feature that controls permission to send (for viewing and changing) the presentation to specified e-mail addresses. To activate this for the current presentation, select **Permission**, and then **Do Not Distribute**, then enter the names or e-mail addresses of people you want to give permission. This means that you will not inadvertently allow your presentation to go to the wrong people and the ability to change the contents can be restricted.

Package for CD

A presentation can be saved on a CD so that it can be used on any computer whether it has **PowerPoint** installed or not (provided the operating system is **Windows 98 Second Edition** or later, e.g. **XP**).

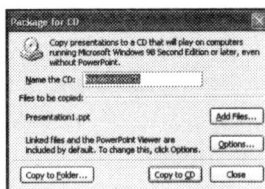

If you have used fonts in your presentation, which may not be present on the host computer, then you can embed them into the presentation (within **Options**).

Web Page Preview

This displays the slides as they appear within a web browser.

Page Setup

The default is on-screen shows, however this be varied if desired using this dialog box.

Print Preview

A new feature for **PowerPoint**, this previews the way the presentations will look when printed (whether slides, handouts or notes pages).

The preview can be changed by pulling down the **Print What** list (located on the toolbar at the top of the screen); the **Options** button displays additional features.

Send To

Use this to send a file to various places, e.g. to an e-mail address for review, in this case the default e-mail editor is automatically opened with the presentation added as an attachment.

Properties

This displays screens of information about the file (some of which can be altered).

Edit menu

	Can't Undo	Ctrl+Z
↺	Repeat Copy	Ctrl+Y
✂	Cut	Ctrl+X
▦	Copy	Ctrl+C
▦	Office Clipboard...	
▦	Paste	Ctrl+V
	Paste Special...	
	Paste as Hyperlink	
	Clear	Del
	Select All	Ctrl+A
	Duplicate	Ctrl+D
	Delete Slide	
▣	Find...	Ctrl+F
	Replace...	Ctrl+H
	Go to Property...	
	Links...	
	Object	

Cut, Copy and Paste

Text or images can be **Cut**, **Copy** or **Paste**(d), using the appropriate buttons on the toolbar.

Office Clipboard

By pulling down the **Edit** menu, followed by **Office Clipboard**, the contents of the clipboard will be displayed in the **Task** pane (on the right of the screen).

By selecting any item, you can **Paste** it into the current slide (*or* by clicking the arrow on the side, **Delete** or **Paste** the item into the current slide), this means any item from the clipboard can be pasted (not just the most recent).

Paste Special

This is similar to the **Paste** command but gives you more control over the format and allows the item to be linked to the original application.

Tip

If **Paste Link** is selected, the object will be *automatically* updated whenever the original is changed.

Paste as Hyperlink

Use this to copy and paste text or objects as hyperlinks.

For example, you may want to paste another slide title (into the present slide) as a hyperlink to that slide, so that if the viewer clicks on the hyperlink then they can jump to that slide.

You can also link to web sites by highlighting text (or selecting an image) and clicking the **Insert Hyperlink** button.

Clear

Selecting this will clear (delete) the selected object or highlighted text.

Select All

This selects all the items (text and objects) on a particular slide, or if in **Slide Sorter View** will select all the slides.

Duplicate

This allows you to duplicate a slide so that an identical copy is added to the presentation (next to the original). Select the required slide, pull down the **Edit** menu, and click on **Duplicate** (it only works in **Slide Sorter View**).

Delete Slide

Pull down the **Edit** menu and choose **Delete Slide**, to delete the current slide (or the selected slide(s) in **Slide Sorter View**).

A slide can also be deleted in **Slide Sorter View** by selecting the slide(s) and pressing the **Del** key.

Tip

Use the **Undo** button if you *quickly* realise you have deleted the slide(s) accidentally.

Find

A standard text tool, this enables you to find words or parts of words within your presentation.

Enter the word or phrase you are looking for and click on the **Match case** and/or **Find whole words only**.

Click on the **Find Next** button and the first occurrence of the word will be found. Then move to the next by clicking on the **Find Next** button and so on.

Tip

Use **Shift** and **F4** to repeat the search.

Replace

This replaces a word or phrase with another.

Links

This displays a dialog box that lets you alter the links. This option is not available until you have selected a linked object within your presentation, i.e. a link created using **Paste Link**.

Objects/Text

Edit objects/text by selecting the item and pulling down the **Edit** menu followed by **Objects** (or more quickly by double-clicking the mouse on the object).

View menu

Normal
Slide Sorter
Slide Show   F5
Notes Page
Master   ▶
Color/Grayscale   ▶
☑ Task Pane   Ctrl+F1
Toolbars   ▶
Ruler
Grid and Guides...
Header and Footer...
Markup
Zoom...

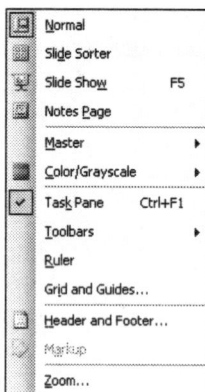

Color/Grayscale

This enables the slides to be viewed in greyscale, colour or black and white.

Task Pane

This displays/hides the pane on the right-hand side of the screen – the contents of the **Task Pane** change depending upon the task in hand.

Toolbars

Adds or removes any toolbars, to do this, pull down the **View** menu and select **Toolbars,** selecting or deselecting the different choices.

To move a toolbar on the screen, move the mouse pointer to the beginning of the toolbar (the cursor becomes an arrow headed cross) and then drag it to a new position.

Once a toolbar is selected, change the shape by moving the mouse pointer along an edge until it becomes a two-headed arrow that is dragged to produce a new shape.

Ruler

Display the vertical and horizontal rulers by selecting this option.

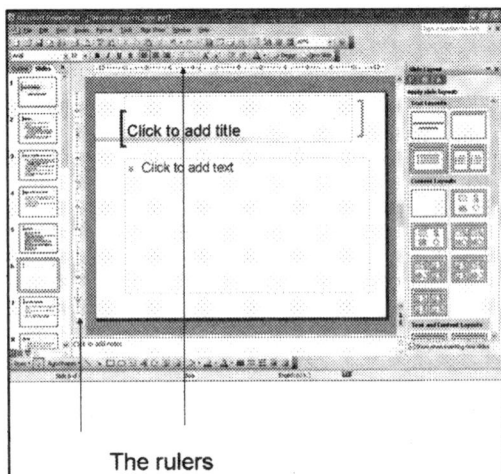

The rulers

Grid and Guides

Display or hide the guides by using the **View** menu and then **Grid and Guides**.

Guides are useful to position objects or text and they can be moved horizontally or vertically by clicking the mouse pointer on the guide and dragging it.

You can display either or both on screen by selecting the option **Display on screen**.

Header and Footer

Insert the date and time, slide numbers and footers onto the slide (either an individual slide or a **Master** slide) by typing in the text.

The **Notes and Handouts** option does the same for the notes and handout pages (headers are unavailable on slides but are enabled on notes and handouts).

Markup

This hides/displays any comments you have added to the slide. Comments are inserted into a slide by pulling down the **Insert** menu, followed by **Comments**.

Insert menu

New Slide	Ctrl+M	
Duplicate Slide		
Slide Number		
Date and Time...		
Symbol...		
Comment		
Slides from Files...		
Slides from Outline...		
Picture	▶	
Diagram...		
Text Box		
Movies and Sounds	▶	
Chart...		
Table...		
Object...		
Hyperlink...	Ctrl+K	

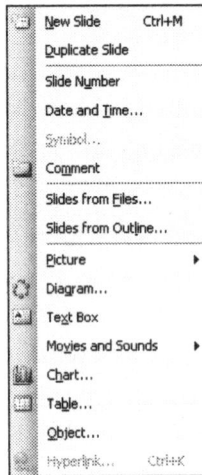

Duplicate Slide

This creates a copy of the current slide and inserts it into the slide show. Useful if you are only making minor alterations to a slide.

Slide Number / Date and Time

An alternative to the use of the **Header and Footer** command (**View** menu) to insert page numbers and dates on the **Master** or on individual slides.

Symbol

You can insert symbols from a variety of character sets into a **text box** within a slide.

The dialog box contains pull-down lists to provide a variety of different fonts and symbols.

To add a symbol, choose the symbol and then click the **Insert** button, followed by **Close.**

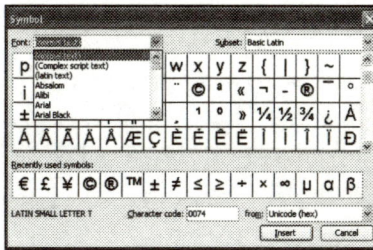

Comment

To insert comments into your slides select this option and type in the comment.

To view the comment, click the button that will appear when you look at the slide in **Normal View**.

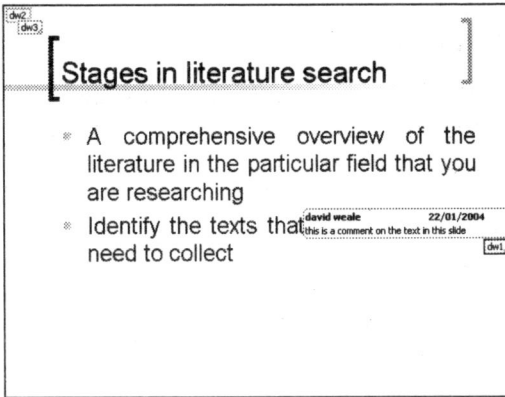

The comments are for your information; they do not appear when you run the **Slide Show** or print out **Handouts**.

Slides from Files

Add slides from another file into your current presentation. To do this, pull down the **Insert** menu and select **Slides from Files**.

In the dialog box, select the file and then the slides you want to add. The new slides will be added after the current slide, and the other slides will be re-sequenced.

Tip

You may find it easiest to use **Slide Sorter View** and position the cursor where you want the new slides to be added.

Slides from Outline

PowerPoint will automatically create a slide show from an outline, using the outline levels as a guide, the first level text is treated as a heading and so on.

For example, if you created an outline within Word you could use this to create a **PowerPoint** presentation without having to retype the text. This works rather effectively and can be a real time-saver.

To do this, pull down the **Insert** menu and select **Slides from Outline**. Find the file you want to use and **PowerPoint** will convert it into a presentation. You will then need to make any alterations and to customise the presentation.

Picture

These are treated in a very similar way to **Clip Art**; they can (mostly but not always, depending upon the type of file) be sized, re-coloured, grouped and ungrouped and so on. Most of these options are available as buttons on the various toolbars – which is quicker than using the menus.

Scanned images require a large amount of disc space to store and tend to slow the system when used.

A partial fix for this is to scale the scanned image before saving it so that it is the correct size. However, you should not make it too small as subsequently increasing the size of an image can reduce the definition.

The type of file you use to save the image will affect the file size; some graphic formats create considerably smaller files (sometimes with a loss of quality depending upon the level of compression).

Tip

To minimise file size, reduce the resolution of your pictures, for viewing on screen 96 dpi as this is the screen resolution; however for printing 160 dpi or more is necessary.

In order of compression (greatest first, although this depends upon the type of image and the quality you need).

□ JPEG & PNG

□ GIF

□ BMP & TIFF

To insert a picture, pull down the **Insert** menu, select **Picture** and then select the type of image from the list.

Diagram

Use this to insert specialised diagrams into a presentation (an alternative to using the specific **Slide Layout**), for example, to insert an **Organisation Chart**.

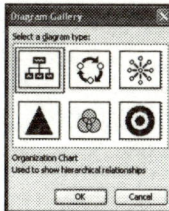

Text Box

To create a textbox use this menu option or click the **Text Box** button (**Drawing** toolbar) and then click and drag to create the box, adding text as desired (which can then be selected, formatted, coloured and so on).

Movies and Sounds

To insert a movie, e.g. from the **Clip Organizer**, is similar to any other media, however in this version of the program, a connection can be made to the Microsoft website and clips can be inserted and/or copied to the hard disc (select the image and click the arrowed bar on the right of the image).

Add sounds in a similar way. You will be asked whether you want the sound to play automatically or when clicked.

You can change the way in which movies and sounds are played by pulling down the **Slide Show** menu and selecting **Custom Animation**.

Format menu

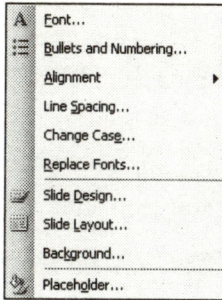

Font

You can alter the font by using the toolbar buttons, however pulling down the **Format** menu and then **Font**, offers more choice.

Bullets and Numbering

To alter the bullets (you can make these changes for an individual slide, or for all the slides by altering the **Master Slide**), select the text for which you want to alter the bullets and then pull down the **Format** menu and select **Bullets**.

An alternative to the menu is to use the toolbar buttons.

There are various options.

You can choose bullets from any character set (**Customize**) or a picture (**Picture**). The **Picture** option contains an **Import** button to import any image to use as a bullet.

The numbering tab also allows changes to be made to the look and feel of the paragraph numbers).

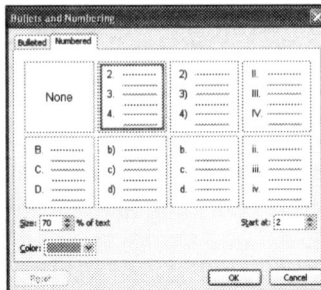

Alignment

To alter the alignment of paragraph(s), highlight the text and then pull down the **Format** menu and select **Alignment**, or use the alignment buttons on the toolbar.

The **Alignment** menu gives more choice than the toolbar (it includes **Justification**).

Alternatively, you can use the following keys (holding the first down while depressing the latter).

CTRL E	centre
CTRL J	justify
CTRL L	left
CTRL R	right

Line Spacing

Hitting the **Return** key will create space; unfortunately, it will also create another bullet. To avoid this, hold down the **Shift** key while depressing the **Return** key, this is a *soft return* and does not give rise to a new bullet.

A more satisfactory way to alter the line spacing (for an individual slide or for the master slide) is to use the **Format** menu and then **Line Spacing**.

You **must** highlight the text to alter the line spacing for more than one line.

A dialog box will appear and you can alter the line spacing and the space before and after paragraphs as you wish, **Preview** the effect on screen as you make the changes.

Tip

Grab the dialog box and move it out of the way, so that you can see the effect more clearly when you **Preview**.

Change Case

You can change the case of the text you have typed.

Believe me this is very useful; it is very easy to type text with the **Caps Lock** key on by mistake.

To use this feature you need to highlight the text and then pull down the **Format** menu and select **Change Case**.

Tip

Use **Shift** and **F3** to alter the case of highlighted text.

Replacing Fonts

In the **Format** menu is an option called **Replace Fonts**, this lets you alter one font to another.

Slide Design

This displays the **Slide Design** pane on the right side of the screen, the same effect can be achieved using the **Design** button on the **Formatting** toolbar.

Background

Pull down the **Format** menu and select **Background**.

Choose another colour and **Preview** or **Apply** it to your slides.

Be careful with the buttons **Apply to All** and **Apply**, depending upon whether you want to change the background of all the slides or not.

Tip

Ticking the **Omit background graphics** option removes any graphics or text that have been included in the **Master Slide**.

Placeholder

Placeholders are the dotted line/boxes holding titles, body text and so on, this option allows the formatting of these, e.g. putting borders around them, colouring the inside to a different colour to the rest of the slide – to make the contents more obvious.

Format Painter

This button (not available within the menus) enables the copying of formatting from one object/text to another.

To work with the **Format Painter**, click on the text/object you want to copy the formatting from, then click on the **Format Painter** button and drag the mouse pointer over the text/object to which you want to copy the attributes.

Tools menu

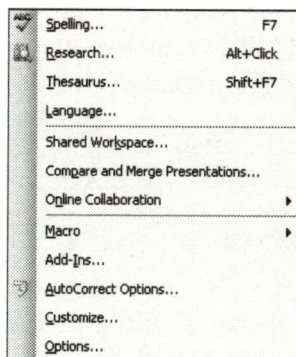

Research

Select this option to connect to a variety of web sites, which will be searched for the keyword. There is a pull-down list **All Reference Books** to narrow the choices (to research a word within a slide, pressing the **Alt** key while clicking the word will have the same effect).

Thesaurus

This suggests alternative words to the one selected on the slide (holding down the **Shift** key while pressing the **F7** key achieves the same result).

Language

Use this to set the language (for spelling and other checking purposes). The default is the choice of language you made when you installed **Windows** (to alter the default, choose another language from the list and click the **Default** button).

Shared Workspace

This is an area on a web server where documents and data can be shared with other workers or friends (it is very useful for group projects). A shared workspace can contain documents, task lists, links, etc.

Compare and Merge Presentations

This option merges another presentation with the current one. It works with a presentation that has been reviewed by another person (after having been sent to that person using **File**, **Send to**).

After the file has been received back by the sender then the two versions can be compared and merged.

In addition, two versions of the same presentation can be compared (without having been reviewed).

The **Revisions** pane is used to accept or reject changes to the original.

The two versions are compared and the toolbar buttons can be used to vary the presentations, incorporating or removing the revisions as desired.

Online Collaboration

This enables the setting up of online meetings to allow discussions to take place (using a web server, either the Internet or an Intranet).

Macro

A macro (in its simplest form) is a series of commands, keystrokes and other activities. You record this series and then play it back without having to enter the keystrokes individually.

Recording and running a macro

To record a macro you can use the **Macro Recorder**.

☐ Pull down the **Tools** menu; select **Macro**, then **Record New Macro**.

☐ Add the Macro name.

☐ Click **OK** and begin to record the macro (carry out the series of keystrokes you wish to record).

☐ When finished, pull down the **Tools** menu and select **Macro**, followed by **Stop Recording**.

☐ To run the macro, pull down the **Tools** menu, select **Macro** and then **Macros**. You will see a dialog box listing the macros.

☐ Select the macro you want to use and click the **Run** button.

In order to run the macro, the file containing the macro has to be open.

Assigning a macro to a toolbar button

Assign a macro to a button on any visible toolbar by pulling down the **Tools** menu and selecting **Customize**, followed by **Commands** and **Macros**.

In the **Categories** list find **Macros** and drag the **macro** onto any of the visible toolbars.

Running a macro during a slide show

☐ On the slide, select the text or object, e.g. an **action button**; you want to use to run the macro.

☐ On the **Slide Show** menu, click **Action Settings**.

☐ In the dialog box, choose either the **Mouse Click** tab or the **Mouse Over** tab, depending upon how you want the macro to be activated.

☐ Click **Run macro**, and then select the macro you want from the list (the list will only contain macros that have been saved within this presentation file).

Add-Ins

These are additional programs, which enhance the use of **PowerPoint**. These add-in programs can be obtained from a variety of sources, e.g. Microsoft's web site.

AutoCorrect Options

This sets rules for **AutoCorrect**.

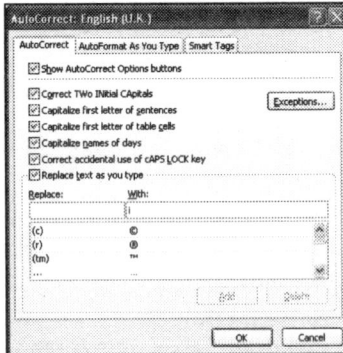

You can make any alterations you want, delete rules, add rules, and create exceptions to the rules and so on.

Customize

Buttons can be added and deleted from the toolbars to reflect the way you personally work.

Pull down the **Tools** menu, select **Customize** and select from the different toolbars shown.

Add buttons by selecting the **Commands** tab and then grabbing the button and dragging it to any toolbar on the screen. To remove a button, simply drag it off the toolbar.

Tip

If you decide that you have made a mess of any toolbar then the **Reset** button on the **Toolbar** menu lets you put everything back to its default position.

Options

In the **Tools** menu is **Options**. This is where various changes to the way the program works can be made.

Each of the tabs (**View, General, and Edit**) contains program settings that you can alter from the default.

Slide Show menu

🖳	View Show	F5
	Set Up Show...	
🔊	Rehearse Timings	
	Record Narration...	
	Action Buttons	▶
	Action Settings...	
📊	Animation Schemes...	
📊	Custom Animation...	
📊	Slide Transition...	
📊	Hide Slide	
	Custom Shows...	

View Show

This runs the slide show; however, it is quicker to
use the **Slide Show** button instead (bottom left of
the screen).

Set Up Show

This option gives various choices on how to run the show
and add flexibility – note the **Performance** section (and
Tips), this can speed/optimise the slide show.

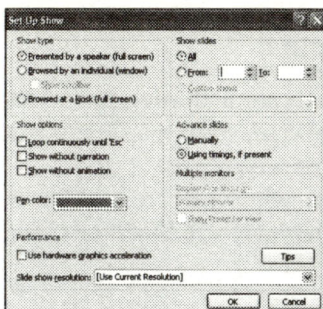

Rehearse Timings

This runs the slide show, rehearsing the timings set, or timings can be set using this option.

To set timings using the **Rehearse Timings** option, use the dialog box (**Rehearsal**) which counts the actual time each slide is viewed and cumulatively the whole slide show. These timings can be used to automate the slide show (for example, where the computer is left running the slide show in a continuous loop at an exhibition).

Use the arrow symbol to advance the slides and the **Repeat** and **Pause** buttons as appropriate. When finished, you will be asked if you want to save the new timings.

Once you have set the timings, use the **Set Up Show** dialog box to alter the **Advance slides** to **Using timings, if present**.

Record Narration

If there is a sound card and microphone attached, a spoken commentary can be added to the slide show.

This can be done while the presentation is running (with audience participation if you wish) or at some other time.

Action Buttons

Add buttons to your slides, which are activated either by clicking the mouse on them or by moving the mouse over them (choices made in the dialog box).

The button can carry out any action defined in the dialog box, e.g. run a program, play a sound or jump to a stated hyperlink (which can be another slide or an Internet/Intranet page).

Choose the button from the display and then click and drag the mouse to create the button within the slide, entering data in the dialog box that will (automatically) appear.

Action Settings

This only becomes available when an action button has been created. You can then change the settings after selecting the button.

Animation Schemes

This displays the **Slide Design** pane on the right of the screen and gives a choice of animations to apply to your slide show.

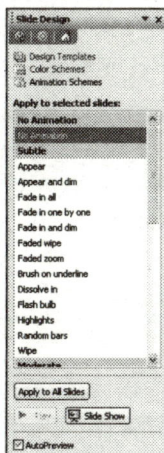

Animations are special effects that can be applied to text, graphics, buttons, etc. When you run your slide show, you will see the animation take place (note the **AutoPreview** button at the bottom), the animation can be applied to all the slides (**Apply to All Slides**) or just to the slide being viewed.

Tip

Too many different animations can lead to the viewer paying more attention to the technique and not enough attention to your message.

Custom Animation

This gives more control over the animations; the **Custom Animation** pane is displayed on the right of the screen.

Select which parts of the slide to animate, in what order the animations take place and whether the animation is automatic or on a mouse-click.

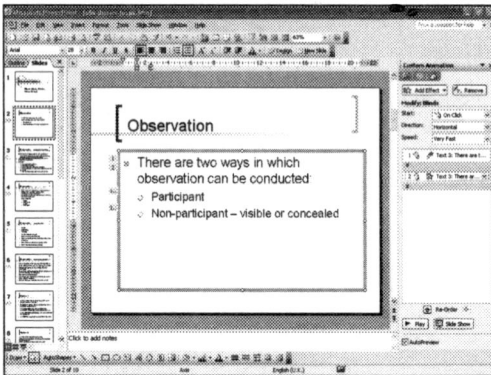

To apply an animation, firstly select the part of the slide, e.g. the text area, an image, etc. Click the **Add Effect** button and select the effect you require.

Once an effect has been selected, then various features can be changed, e.g. **Start**, **Speed**, etc.

Tip

If you want the same animation effect to appear on every slide, then apply the required effects to the **Master Slide**

Dimming text (line by line)

One of the most successful special effects is to alter the colour of each line of text (as the next line appears), so that the current line appears in a prominent colour and the previous points are dimmed, the audience is therefore concentrating on the current point that is being made.

Select the item by clicking it in the **Custom Animation** pane (to select multiple items, hold down the **Ctrl** key and click the mouse).

Click the arrow to the right of the item(s), and select **Effect Options** and then **Effect**. Finally, choose the effects, e.g. change the text colour in the **After animation** box.

Slide Transition

This is a special effect as one slide disappears and the next appears. To set this, select the **Slide Show** menu and then **Slide Transition**.

Select the transition from the list and alter the options as you wish, the effect is shown as the changes are made. The transition can be applied to all the slides or only to the current slide.

Within this pane, it is possible to set the slide show to run automatically using set timings for the slides **Advance slide** (**Automatically after**), e.g. for an exhibition. The slide timings can also be set manually using the **Set Up Show** option within the **Slide Show** menu.

Hide Slide

This hides individual slides so that they do not display.

If you are in **Slide Sorter View**, it is possible to select several slides (hold down the **Ctrl** key while clicking the mouse pointer on each).

To hide a slide, select the slide(s), pull down the **Tools** menu and select **Hide Slide**, or if in **Slide Sorter View** use the **Hide Slide** button (on the upper toolbar).

Displaying Hidden Slides

Type the character **H** while displaying the previous slide.

When printing, the dialog box is set to print the hidden slides (the default) or by removing the tick, print the slides without including the hidden slides.

Custom Shows

This option allows the creation of slide shows that contain (some of the) slides from the original slide show.

You may want to do this because you are dealing with a variety of audiences, each of which requires a different version of the original.

Click on **New** and then you will see the following dialog box. Choose the slides and then **Add** them to the custom show.

Help menu

Microsoft PowerPoint Help

This displays the **Help** pane on the right of the screen, use it to obtain assistance on any topic that needs clarity or explanation (pressing the **F1** key has the same effect).

Tip

It is often sensible to print out these topics, so there is a printed record for reference in the future and to use while addressing the problem (switching between the **Help** screen and the program is not as easy).

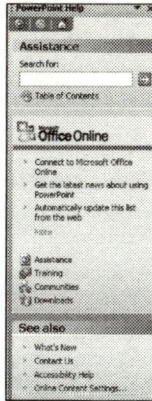

Show the Office Assistant

This is an animation – my favourite is the wizard. Left-clicking the figure displays a prompt asking what is required, right-clicking allows various choices (described below).

Assistant Choices

After right-clicking the mouse button on the assistant and selecting **Options**, a dialog box appears which enables you to choose a different assistant (**Gallery**).

Alternatively, if you select the **Options** tab, you can make various changes.

Microsoft Office Online

This option will connect to the **Microsoft** site on the Internet.

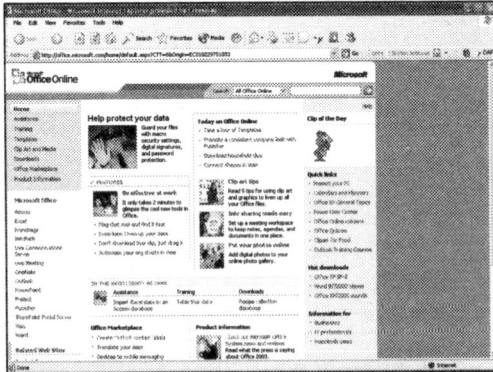

Contact Us

This also connects to the **Microsoft** web site, displaying contact details.

Check for Updates

Similarly, this connects the site and checks for any new features, etc.

It is sensible to do this on a regular basis as **Microsoft** regularly adds functionality to its programs.

Customer Feedback Options

This enables automatic notification of updates, new templates, etc. It is also possible to join the global community in providing feedback on the program and thereby improving it.

About Microsoft PowerPoint

This displays information about the program.

The tutorial

After opening the program, click the **New** button (top left on the **Standard** toolbar). The screen should look like this.

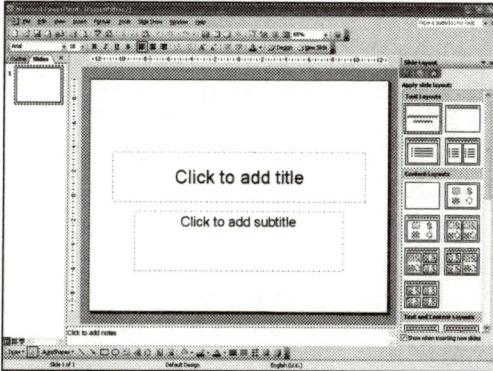

Entering Text

Enter the following title (click the mouse within the existing text to begin).

My Slide Show

Enter the following subtitle:

Using PowerPoint

My Slide Show

Using PowerPoint

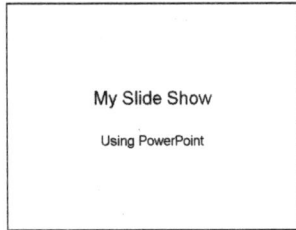

This is the initial slide, now to add slides, click on the **New Slide** button.

The **Title and Text** layout should automatically be chosen (if not, click the **Text Layout** button).

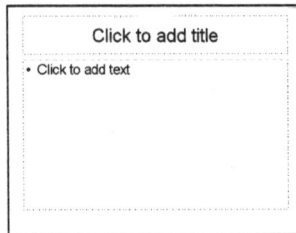

Click to add title

• Click to add text

Add the following title:

The First Slide

Add the text:

Line One

Press the **return** key and then enter the following lines, pressing **return** between each:

Line Two

Line Three

Line Four

```
                    The First Slide
          • Line One
          • Line Two
          • Line Three
          • Line Four
```

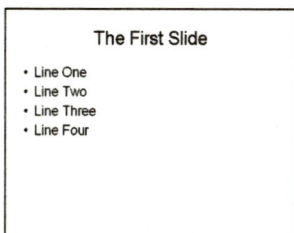

Click on the **New Slide** button and again choose the **Title and Text** layout.

Add the following title:

The Second Slide

Add the text (exactly as spelt).

Line Fiive

Line Siix

Line Sevenn

Line Ate

Line Nine

You have now created three slides.

Saving your work

It is best to save your work regularly.

To do so, click on the **Save** button, click in the
File name box and name your file *Present1*.

Save it to the folder of your choice.

Text editing

Use the double-headed arrows on the bottom right of the screen to move back to the initial slide (titled *My Slide Show*), the **Pg Up** keys achieve the same objective.

Now we will alter the font. To do so, highlight the text by clicking and dragging the mouse, then pull down the **Font** list (**Formatting toolbar** – top left of the screen).

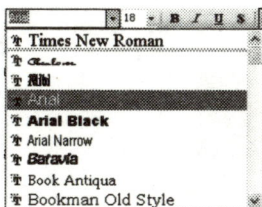

Alter the *title* font to **Comic Sans MS 54 pt** and the *subtitle* to the same font and **44 pt size** (use the **Font Size** list next to the **Font** list).

Use the double-arrow buttons to move to the next slide (titled *The First Slide*).

Change the size of the title (of this slide) to **Comic Sans MS 54 pt** and the text to **Times New Roman 44 pt**.

Move to the final slide and alter the fonts in the same way.

Move back to the slide titled *The First Slide* (actually the second slide, not the title slide).

Select the body text (Line One, etc.), by highlighting it. Then pull down the **Format** menu and then **Line Spacing**.

Alter the **Before Paragraph** to **0.5** and then click on the **Preview** button. If satisfactory click on **OK**.

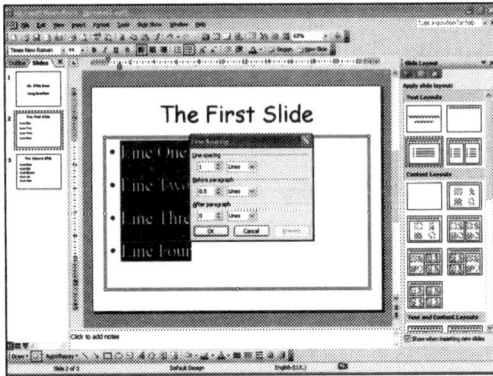

Make sure the text is selected, use the **Center** button on the toolbar to centre the text (this centres each line between the margins of the slide).

Move to the final slide (titled *The Second Slide*) and highlight the body text.

From the **Format** menu select **Bullets and Numbering**, then **Customize**, and select **Wingdings** from the **Font** list. Choose a new bullet, then alter the various options (**Color**, **Size** and so on), and finally click on **OK**.

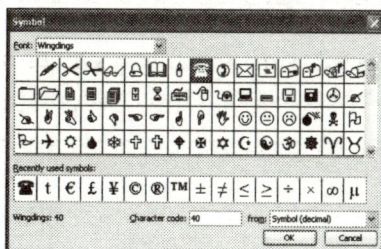

Do this again, this time choosing a sensible bullet.

You now need to use the **Drawing** toolbar. This should be displayed along the bottom of the screen, however if it is not then pull down the **View** menu, select **Toolbars** and then **Drawing**.

The toolbar looks like this.

Make sure the text is still highlighted and then use the **Font Color** button on the **Drawing** toolbar to colour the text *Blue* (click on the arrow to the right of the button and then select **More Colors**).

Now just highlight the word *Sevenn* and change its colour to *Black*.

Move back to the first slide (titled *My Slide Show*) and select the subtitle by clicking to display the text border.

From the **Draw** menu (**Drawing** toolbar), choose **Rotate or Flip** and then **Free Rotate**.

Grab one of the corners of the text border and rotate the text. Grab the text and drag it further down the slide.

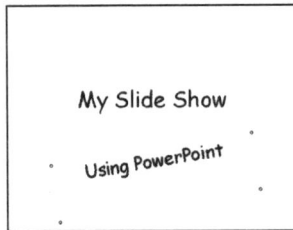

```
My Slide Show

    Using PowerPoint
```

Finally click on the **Spelling** button and spell-check your slides, correcting as necessary.

You have various options; you can **Ignore** or **Ignore All** (occurrences of the word), **Change** to the correct spelling or **Add** to the dictionary.

Save the file.

Remember that the spellchecker may identify a word that is correct but not within its dictionary. The spell check did not pick up the word *Ate* in the final slide. You will need to alter this manually.

Transitions

The transition effect (this alters the way in which each slide is loaded onto the screen) is very effective in making the presentation more professional.

Click on the **Slide Sorter View** button (bottom left of the screen).

The slides are all shown (as miniatures).

Tip

Use the **Zoom** button to see them all if there are too many to fit on the screen initially.

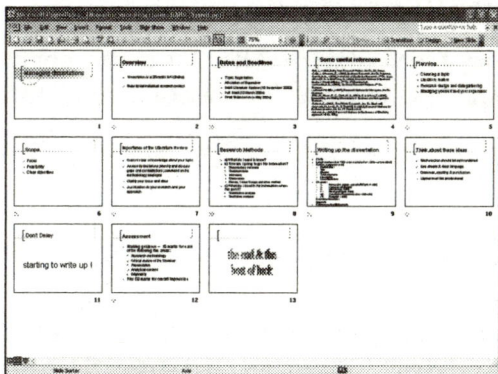

Use the **Slide Transition** button to create
a transition; the **Slide Transition** pane is
shown on the right of the screen.

At least one slide has to be selected (clicked) in order to do
this.

The different effects are displayed as you choose the
transitions. You can alter the speed of the transition
(**Modify Transition**), I suggest you begin with **Slow**.

Alternatively, pull down the **Slide Show** menu and select
Slide Transition to display the pane.

Finally, click on the **Apply to All Slides** button.

Animations

With at least one slide selected, you can apply special
effects to the way in which the lines of text are displayed.

Pull down the **Slide Show** menu and select **Animation
Schemes**.

The animations are displayed in the pane on the right of the
screen.

Select the animation you want to use and click the **Apply
to All Slides** button.

Select the first slide in the series and click on the **Slide Show** button along the bottom left of the screen and use the left-hand mouse button to advance the text and slides.

Tip

Practise altering the **Transition** and **Animation**, so you can see the effect of the different techniques.

Looking at your Slides

Slide Sorter

Click on the **Slide Sorter** button. You will see all
the slides together.

You have already used this to produce transitions and
animations for the slide show; another use is to rearrange
the slides.

The next technique will not work if the slides are all still
selected; if they are still all selected, click the cursor away
from them.

Now grab the last slide with the mouse and drag it in front
of the first slide (you will see a line appear where the slide
will be moved to).

Now move it back.

Use the **Normal View** button to return to the slides.

Printing the slides

You can print your slides:

☐ One to a page onto paper or you can print them onto transparencies directly using a colour ink-jet printer.

☐ Up to nine to a page so you can issue them as handouts to your audience.

To print, pull down the **File** menu, select **Print**, and select the options you require.

Save the file.

Tip

If you want to save the file under a different name or to a different directory, you need to pull down the **File** menu and then choose **Save As**.

Slide Designs

You can add a background design to your slides (and this is normally recommended) by clicking the **Design** button and then applying a **Design Template**.

The designs are shown in the pane on the right of the screen; choose the design you want to apply by scrolling down the list.

Click the arrow to the right of the image and select from the options.

Tip

It is best to apply a design at the start of the slide show, since it may alter any existing fonts and layout.

If you want to change the design simply repeat the process.

Save and close the file (**File, Close**).

Adding Graphics

The fun starts. Used sensibly, graphics add to a presentation.

Start a new file (click on the **New** (file) button on the left of the upper toolbar), choose a **Blank** (**Layout**).

Clip Art

Then pull down the **Insert** menu, **Picture** and then **Clip Art** or use the button on the **Drawing** toolbar.

Enter a word in the **Search** box (on the right of the screen) and then click the chosen image, selecting **Insert** from the list of choices.

The picture will appear within the slide. Do not worry about its size or position at present.

WordArt

Create a second slide (**New Slide** button) and select the **Blank** (**Layout**).

Select the **Insert WordArt** button (**Drawing** toolbar; if it is not shown, pull down the **View** menu, select **Toolbars** followed by **Drawing**).

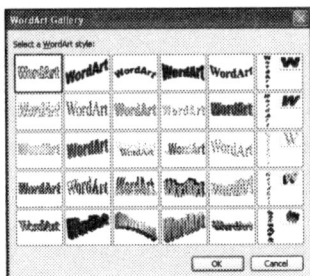

Choose a format and click **OK**.

Enter the following text (by overtyping the original text) and click the **OK** button.

Fancy Letters

Remember if you want to alter it afterwards, click the mouse on the text and **WordArt** toolbar will be loaded automatically, you can then use the various buttons to create effects.

Your finished slide may look like this.

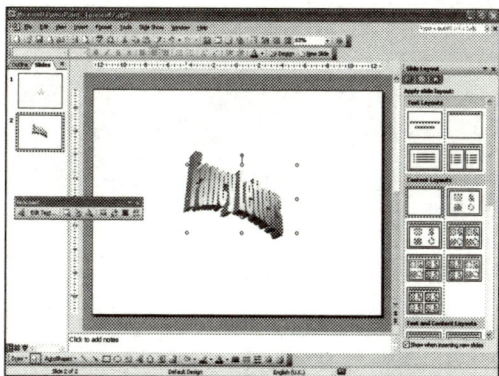

Save the file as *Present2*.

Organisation Charts

Click on the **New Slide** button and then select the **Organisation Chart** layout (shown in the following illustration in the **Layout** pane).

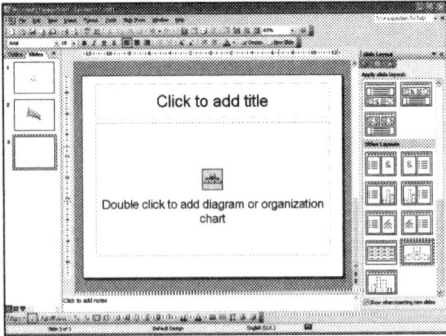

Double-clicking the image displays a choice of charts, select the first. The module will appear.

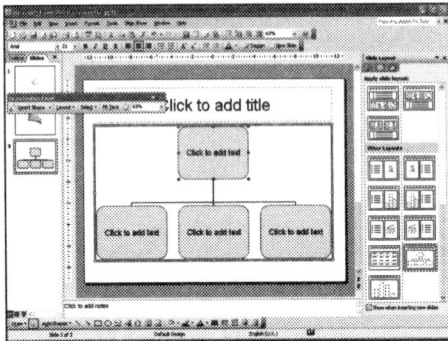

Click on the box to the right (lower row) to select it, ensuring that there are small circles around the box and delete it (use the **delete** key).

Click the left-hand box and then on the *arrow* to the right of the **Insert Shape** button (*Organization Chart* toolbar) and select **Subordinate**. This will add the subordinate below that box.

Now add a **Co-worker** box to the side of the **Subordinate** box. The result should look like this.

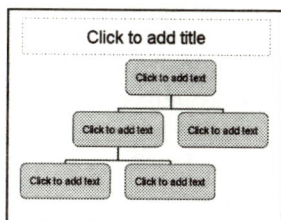

Click the **AutoFormat** button (on the **Organization toolbar**) and select from the choices.

Add the following text to the chart boxes.

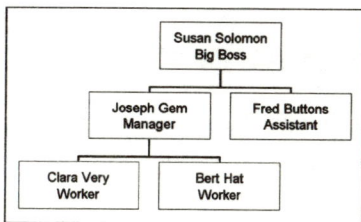

Click in the title area and enter the title:

Swansong PLC

You have created your own customised organisation chart.

Finally, save your file (but do not *close* it).

Borders/Arrows

Insert a picture into the slide; choose a suitable image for Susan. Scale this to a suitable size.

Click on the **Arrow** button (**Drawing** toolbar) and draw an arrow from Susan to the picture.

Tip

Hold the **Shift** key while drawing the arrow, this will ensure it is straight.

With the arrow selected, pull down the **Format** menu and then **Colors and Lines** and alter the line colour and style of the arrow (or you can double-click the arrow).

Now add a picture and arrow for Joseph (the manager). The result may look similar to this.

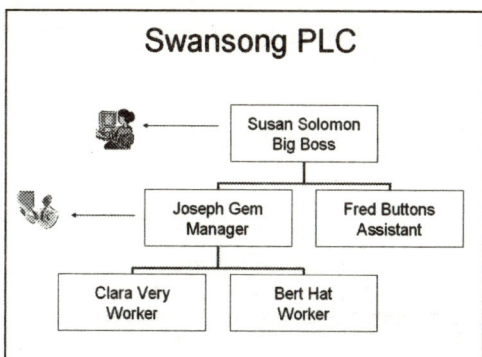

Finally, save the file.

Adding sounds (and movies)

You can add sounds and movies to your slides.

Insert a new slide and select **Title Only** (Layout), this will impose a title area on to the slide.

Add the following title:

Sounds and movies too!

Pull down the Insert menu and then Movies and Sounds followed by Sound from Clip Organizer.

Select a sound; it will appear within the slide as a speaker icon.

You will be given a choice as to whether the sound starts automatically or not.

You can also right-click the icon (selecting **Edit Sound Object**) and make it keep looping (this may become irritating).

Now insert a movie in the same way.

Click the **Slide Show** button and see the effects.

Save and close the file.

Altering Slides

Making changes on the *master slide* will affect all the slides making up the presentation.

Open the first file you created (PRESENT1), using the **Open** button to do so.

Master Slides

View the second slide in the sequence and pull down the **View** menu and then **Master** and finally **Slide Master**.

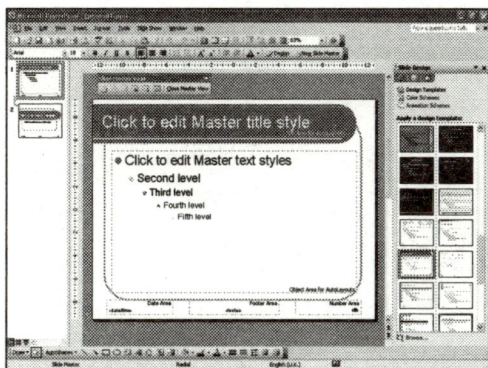

Anything you add to the *master slide* will appear on every slide in the slide show.

Be careful, anything added to the **Title master** will only affect that type of slide and similarly with the **Slide Master**.

Tip

Use the scroll bar (or **Page Up/Page Down** keys) to move from one type to the other, i.e. from **Slide Master** to **Title Master**.

Using the **Slide Master**, highlight *<date/time>* and pull down the **Insert** menu and select **Date and Time**, choose one of these, note the **Update automatically** button.

Highlight the *<footer>* and enter your name.

Click on the **Slide Show** button to display your slides with the time/date and your name shown on each.

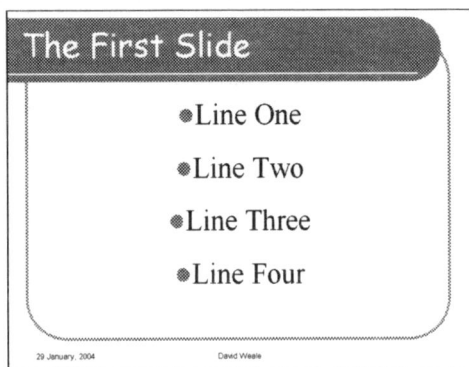

The First Slide

- Line One
- Line Two
- Line Three
- Line Four

29 January, 2004   David Weale

Save and close the file.

Running slide shows automatically

Self-running presentations are useful for exhibitions and displays, as they do not need anyone to be physically present. A self-running presentation can be set to loop repeatedly.

To set up a self-running show: open a presentation; select the **Slide Show** menu, followed by **Set Up Show** and make choices.

Rehearse Timings

This runs the slide show, rehearsing the timings you have set, or you can set timings using this option.

To set the slide show timings use the option **Slide Show** and **Rehearse Timings**.

Use the arrow symbol to advance the slides and the **Repeat** and **Pause** buttons as appropriate. When you have finished, you will be asked if you want to save the new timings.

Once you have set the timings, use the **Set Up Show** dialog box to alter the **Advance slides** to **Using timings, if present**.

Effective presentations

First Things

Decide WHAT you want to achieve

Do you want to impart information or to persuade your audience in some way (e.g. to change their beliefs or attitudes)?

☐ Consider the type of audience you are addressing and what they want from the presentation. Pitch the level of your presentation carefully; audiences vary in their attention span, intellectual ability, etc.

☐ Decide upon the best way to get your message across for the specific audience.

Planning the Material

- ☐ Brainstorm main ideas and then sub-ideas

- ☐ Plan any handouts

- ☐ Plan visual aids

- ☐ Structure presentation with

- ☐ Introduction

- ☐ Body

- ☐ Strong conclusion

- ☐ Write down the main points and then, underneath that the detail.

- ☐ Make use of **Outline** view to enter content. After the content has been added then consider the look and feel of the presentation.

The audience likes to have something to take away, so prepare a handout or a copy of the slides you have used.

Give out handouts before or after a presentation. Personally, I like to give them out at the start so the audience can annotate them; however, there is a danger that the audience will read them rather than listen to you.

Creating a summary slide

It can be useful to create a slide that summarises the presentation. To do so:

☐ Pull down the **View** menu and select **Slide Sorter** or use the button along the bottom of the screen.

☐ Zoom the view and select the slides to include in the summary and then click the **Summary Slide** button. This slide will become the first slide in the presentation.

To select consecutive slides, hold down the **Shift** key and click the first and last slides to be included, to select several non-sequential slides, hold down the **Ctrl** key and click each slide.

The Presentation

Begin with an arresting sentence; close with a strong summary; in between speak clearly, simply and always to the point; and above all be brief. *(William Mayo)*

Always introduce the material (subject, contents) and yourself (background, qualifications) to the audience and wrap it all up at the end by summarising what you have told them and ask for questions (unless you want to deal with questions during the presentation, make it clear at the start which method your prefer).

The sequence of the presentation should be logical, starting simply before developing complex points. A presentation is an overview of the subject and it may be preferable to use handouts for complex details.

The start and end of the presentation are critical to its success, so pay particular attention to these.

Your voice is of primary importance, keep it slow and interested, emphasise the important points and the changes of topic, this keeps your audience awake.

Try to avoid referring to notes or cue cards, as the audience would prefer if you appeared in command of the subject.

Maintain eye contact with as many of the audience as possible.

The audience is most likely to have a worthwhile experience if you exude enthusiasm, seem to be enjoying yourself and (appear to) know your subject.

Consider dress and body language, these can make or mar the overall presentation.

Practise your presentation and revise it until you can present it with ease, possibly using a video camera (which can be scary). The more familiar you are with the material, the better will be the presentation.

The Environment

Always check the room, seating, lighting and the display equipment (computer, OHP, projector, etc.).

Ensure the image and text is bright, in focus and large enough for everyone to see clearly.

Make sure that all the audience can actually see the screen easily (try not to stand in front of it). Arrange the seating and adjust any other environmental features (heating, lighting, etc.) as necessary.

Visuals

Consider starting and ending the presentation with identical slides, summarising the main points.

Keep a consistent style throughout the slides. Use Clip Art, charts or drawings to make points or to amuse but be careful not to detract from the actual message.

Use the design, animation and transition effects to add a degree of professionalism but do be consistent with their use (and any other special effects), as you want the audience to pay attention to the content, **not** to the technology.

Try to avoid complicated images or backgrounds, as these can be confusing to the audience and detract from the points you are trying to put across.

Be aware of contrasts. Dark letters on a light backdrop show up well, charts and diagrams look good with a light (but not too bright) background.

When using visuals, be silent for a few seconds so the audience can absorb the detail, then explain the slide to the audience.

Text

Use initial capital letters but then lower case (i.e. not all capitals).

Keep the number of words, lines, numbers or graphic images to the absolute minimum for each slide (the maximum number of lines should ideally not be more than six).

The slides should contain *key points* or *phrases*; they are not supposed to contain sentences or paragraphs.

Use large fonts for readability; blue/black is easier to read at a distance, use **bold**, $\dot{\text{size}}$ and **colour** to enhance text and use italics sparingly (perhaps for quotes).

If it looks right on the computer screen, it is probably too small for most rooms, it is best to practise in the room (or similar) to check that the person at the back can see the details on each slide. The default font sizes in PowerPoint may not be large enough for your slides; it is timesaving to alter the **Master Slide** or the **template** – so that all the slides will take on the new sizes.

Create a professional finish by ending with a blank coloured slide (or a slide with your company logo) and always **Spell-check**.

Fonts

There are two types of font, *Serif* and *Sans Serif*.

An example of Serif is times new roman, this can be used for body text (note the lines running along the bottom of the characters – this is intended to make it easier to read as the eye follows the lines)

The other is Sans serif, e.g. Arial, which can be used for headings (this has no *serifs*).

You will find that each of the **PowerPoint** designs has its own combination of fonts, which can be changed if you so wish.

Errors

Your presentation will be more successful if you avoid the following mistakes.

☐ Reading rather than speaking to the audience

☐ Speaking too quickly

☐ Too much detail – in too little time

☐ Using confusing jargon or too much complexity of argument

☐ Unreadable graphs/illustrations (when projected)

☐ Over or under-running – timing is critical.

Nervousness

There are two types of speakers: those that are nervous and those that are liars. (*Mark Twain*)

To overcome the inevitable stage fright, try the following tips.

☐ Breathe deeply.

☐ Focus on relaxing, when sitting try to do so comfortably with a straight back.

☐ Try to move around rather than sit throughout the presentation.

☐ Prepare properly.

☐ Do not wear new shoes/clothes and avoid fussy (busy) clothes that draw the audience's attention.

☐ Try visualisation; imagine yourself going through the stages of a successful presentation, this works!

☐ Concentrate on what you are doing, the audience will take care of itself.

Appendices

Office Downloads

Microsoft have developed a large variety of web-based resources, the following illustrations give an idea of the scope of these.

Office Clip Art

There is a wide variety of graphic tools and images available from the Microsoft web site **Clip Art on Office Online**, this is part of **Office Online** and can be accessed directly from within PowerPoint (**Insert Clip Art** and then click the link at the bottom of the **Clip Art** pane).

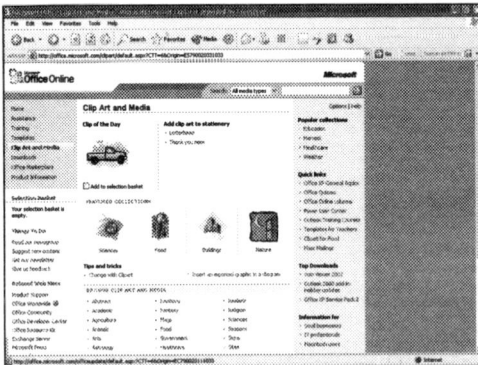

PowerPoint site

This is part of **Office Online** dedicated to PowerPoint and can be accessed through the **Help** pane or from the home page of **Office Online** (available from the **Help** menu).

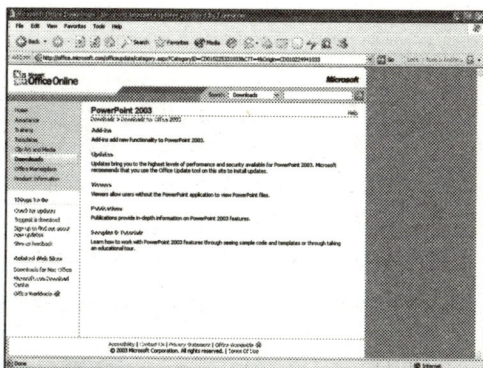

Downloads

Available via the **Office Online** home page, this contains the program fixes, additional add-in programs and other useful **Office** features; this is worthwhile visiting on a regular basis.

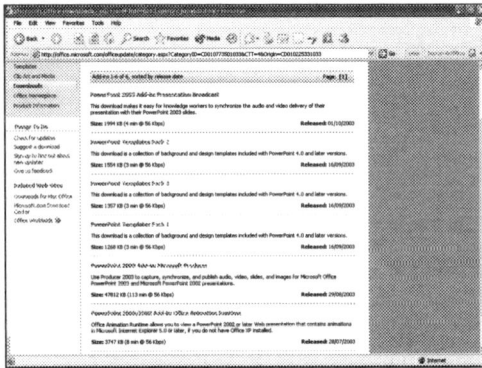

Keyboard Shortcuts

To display keyboard shortcuts in **Tool Tips** (i.e. they will appear when the mouse pointer is over one of the toolbar buttons) pull down the **Tools** menu followed by **Customize** and **Options** tab, and click on **show shortcut keys in screen tips**.

Activity	Shortcut Keys
Bold	CTRL+B
Capitalize	SHIFT+F3
Copy	CTRL+C
Delete (a word)	CTRL+BACKSPACE
Find	CTRL+F
Insert a hyperlink	CTRL+K
Insert a new slide	CTRL+M
Italics	CTRL+I
Make a duplicate of the current slide	CTRL+D
Open	CTRL+O
Paste	CTRL+V
Print	CTRL+P
Repeat the last action	F4
Save	CTRL+S
Select all	CTRL+A
Start a slide show	F5
Subscript	CTRL+EQUAL SIGN (=)
Superscript	CTRL+PLUS SIGN (+)
Undo	CTRL+Z
View guides	CTRL+G

Glossary

Action Buttons	These buttons perform an action when you click them, to start a video, play sounds, or jump to a hyperlink.
Alignment	The position of text or objects, horizontal alignment can be right, left, centred or justified.
Animation Effects	These are builds and other effects that are applied to text (etc.) to make them interesting and prominent, for example to show one line of a slide at a time.
Audience Handouts	Handouts contain miniatures of your slides often printed 6 to a page.
Auto Layouts	Slide layouts with placeholders for titles, text, and objects such as Clip Art, graphs, and charts.
AutoContent Wizard	The *AutoContent Wizard* is a systematic guide to choosing contents, layout design, style, and type.
AutoCorrect	Corrects *common* typing errors, the setting can be customised (*Tools. AutoCorrect Options*).
AutoFit	This automatically resizes text in a slide.
AutoShapes	Shapes that are drawn by clicking the button (for the shape) and dragging.
Background (Fill)	The dialog box provides options to alter the background of slides.
Black-and-White View	Shows how your presentation will look in b&w.
CDR/CDRW	A method of backing up data and moving files. CDR is a writable CD, CDRW is a rewritable CD (one that can be erased and rewritten).

Clipboard	This holds cut or copied items, they can then be pasted into a slide. To view the contents *Edit*, *Office Clipboard*.
Collate	This (*Print* option) ensures that one complete copy of the slides is printed before beginning on the next.
Comments	Texts added to a slide for information, the comments do not appear when the slide is viewed.
Crop	Removing part of an image (it does not delete any of the image but hides the unwanted part).
Default	The program setting unless it is changed to something else, e.g. left alignment is the default alignment setting.
Demote	Moves the text to a lower level of importance within the slide (can be used in *Outline* view).
Dialog box	Displays the commands available, can be interactive and choices made.
Drag-and-drop	Selecting the text and dragging it to a new location.
Drawing Toolbar	Drawing tools include *AutoShapes*, objects can be drawn, coloured, etc.
Embedded object	Images/text inserted into the presentation (often linked to the originating program).
Font Size	A font size measures font size in points (72 points to an inch).
Footer/Header	Information along the bottom of a slide (footer) or top (header) repeated on every page, e.g. page numbers.
GIF/JPEG	Common image formats, they compress the file size (smaller files).

Grid	Horizontal and vertical lines displayed on a slide to make lining up easy.
HTML	The language used for Web pages.
Hyperlink	Text or an image linked to another slide, file, or website.
Landscape/Portrait	The layout of the page, *Landscape* is horizontal orientation. *Portrait* means vertical orientation.
Master slide	Used to create a common look to all the slides, e.g. a company logo or the date, which appears on every slide.
Microsoft Graph	An applet to create charts and graphs (not as sophisticated as using Excel).
Microsoft Organization Chart	Used to create an organization chart (available in any Office application).
Normal view	This view shows the *Outline* tab, *Slide* pane, and *Notes* pane.
Notes Page View	Use this to add notes to individual slides – these can be printed out.
Objects	Any graphic, e.g. text boxes, pictures.
Outline View	Outline view enables the slide titles and main text to be edited. The view can be expanded or collapsed by clicking the + and – buttons.
Placeholders	These are areas on slides where objects or text can be placed (they can be sized by clicking and dragging).
Read-only	These files can only be read, not edited or altered.
Rehearsal Timer	Used to set timings for your slides.
Resize	Change the size of an object (text box or graphic) by dragging the corners.

Rotate (handles)	A small green circle used to rotate the object (pressing *Shift* while rotating moves it in discrete increments).
ScreenTips	An explanation of the purpose of a button that appears when the mouse pointer is moved over it.
Slide Master	This slide holds the current design template such as font style, background.
Slide Sorter View	Displays a small image of all the slides in a grid. Makes some tasks easier, e.g. rearranging, applying transitions.
Slide Transition	This controls how a slide makes its appearance, e.g. Box In.
Speaker's Notes	Speaker's Notes are pages with a copy of a slide in the top half of the page and the notes in the second half of the page.
Templates	Templates can be created using specific backgrounds, designs, fonts, etc.
Text box	Text boxes can be placed anywhere on a slide and contain formatted text, etc.
Thumbnail	A small version of the current slide.
Title slide	The initial slide layout, usually the first slide in the presentation.
Ungrouping	Ungrouping images separates them into their component parts.
WordArt	Text formatted like a graphic, can be used for special effects and/or titles.

Index